TRUE CONFESSIONS

&

FALSE ROMANCES

a book of poems by

WILLIAM HATHAWAY

an Ithaca House *book*

Ithaca

Grateful acknowledgment is made for permission to reprint and assignment of copyright to the following magazines and anthologies in which many of these have appeared: *Abraxas, Doones, Epoch, Foxfire, Hearse, Intro 2,* Bantam Books, 1969, ed. by R. V. Cassill, *The Little Magazine, Minnesota Review, New: American and Canadian Poetry, New England Review, Northeast, Painted Horses, Poetry Northwest, Quickly Aging Here,* ed. by Geof Hewitt, Doubleday Anchor Book, 1969, *Wormwood Review.*

Cover by Thom Burton & Steve Gilbert

ITHACA HOUSE
314 FOREST HOME DRIVE
ITHACA, NEW YORK 14850

for my parents and for my wife

CONTENTS

I

For The Lost Coal Miners

Half sick with excitement
I saw the towns the old conductor
croaked about from car to car.
Sayre, Bethlehem, and in Jim Thorpe
I peered everywhere for real Indians.

But all I saw were dirty buildings
and hills of coal and mountains of slag.
The faces of unhurried, unhappy white
men dismally grouped in a twilit world
of drizzle that moved suddenly grey to
                                    black.

And I recognized that in the T.V. pictures.
But I also thought of faces by Da Vinci,
how you know it isn't Rembrandt by
the eyes and cheekbones, passive hands.
How friendless it is behind the face.

I remembered eating a *sandwich jambon*
with lifeless beer in the Louvre cafeteria.
while a steady rain fell below in the square.
Later in rooms full of battles and cherubs
I went weak with loneliness without a chair.

When a blue sky brings to mind Raoul Dufy
it may as well be your daughter's eye
                                    shadow.
We become very religious in these hard times
and our own hardness is sealing the shaft,
far above us, where people stand sadly in
                                    the rain.

THE CRAZY LADY

The Dirty Man makes an obscene invitation
to the Crazy Lady in the Italian courtyard
of the BPL. Korea she yells, Korea.
That's all you think of. Korea she whispers.
She is very crazy, the Crazy Lady.

Drunks moan in their sleep when the sun
slips them into the shade. The splashing
fountain makes them wet their pants.
Such a peaceful place to sit in the summer,
clean gravel paths and little orange trees.

The Crazy Lady confers with her lawyers.
She bawls them all out, dismisses a few,
then she pleads, weeps and they come back.
She is suing all of us: me, the drunks,
the library guard, the Cuban who fixes

the fountain, even the children and birds.
The Dirty Man pulls at his jug and leers.
He moves with the sun closer to her
dark corner. He shows us what he wants.
His fly is open; he is very dirty, the Dirty Man.

Oh, but there is no cause for alarm.
Every day this happens, see they are lovers.
They hold hands and talk quietly so as
not to disturb. Soon they will go
to the Commons, by the wading pool,

feed squirrels, talk of what they'll
do when she gets all that money.

The Third Day Of Christmas

*"Home is the place where, when you have
to go there,
They have to take you in."*

                                        Robert Frost

The sofa is broken
and the relatives who sent me
there are snoring with fearsome noise.
Also the wind
is clapping the T.V. cable to the house,
the cat
is raising hell with styrofoam packing
material in the utility room
I get up
and kick the cat, because I can't do
much about anything else.
While I'm at it
I have a whiskey
and another
and on some nutty impulse
I decide to shovel the driveway.
It is nutty
because it's freezing outside
and the shovel makes a racket.
Jogging around
the block I look up to see the moon
and the men whirling around it.
But of course
there isn't any moon.
So I go back
and kick the cat and have a whiskey,
wake up everyone accidentally.
It's my house,
though, they can't do anything.

When Beulah Did The Hula In Missoula

Snow in August, and people
talking about it all the way
up to the cheap hotel which
wasn't cheap and smelled like
popcorn; gas leaked somewhere.

Nothing moves that mountain
but weather and earthworms.
Signs say pack a shovel, pail,
axe, beware of grizzly bears.
It's a long way from Raspail.

A bad place to camp, much less
mate, where game are counted,
tagged, and Indians stay drunk.
At Chenonceaux the river doesn't
run but history is *son et lumiere*.

When fires come they grab men
off the streets, mills close,
Smokey waves from the bank.
An Indian tosses coals to forest
muttering burn, you mother, burn.

Where Racine is not Wisconson
there are cuckolds and baroque
ladies leaning on their pillars.
Now, held behind the gills,
my bug-eyes trout mouths,
help, I'm starving, oh God.

ITHACA

When ice leaves the shale
a little looser, town earth
along the sidewalks stinks
of dogshit and woods
have a cemetery smell
under the dripping limbs.

I've lived here for years,
inching across the valley walls,
a small dot in the lake.
On a calm late August night
over an open fire it's not uncommon
to see the winter forming in my eyes.

There are those hereabouts who
estimate offhandedly the years
I've had, and still have left.
As we shuffle, deal, and pass
the rain is steady on the lawn,
our jokes dry, weightless noise.

In the photographs I'm skinny,
always twisted in some laughter.
Half-naked in the maple shade
or embracing a snow woman,
always a loose face at my shoulder
grins as if the pose has been too long.

It's love makes me do it.
Dry teeth in the gorge bottom
nor the bitter ways of my children
can change this sweet, sweet taste.
Listen to the snow and the soft
persistent rap of knuckles on oak bark.

WALLACE

I've let you get away with every-
thing. The girl, ranch, the whole
shebang. And I'm drinking soup
in Wallace, Idaho, while a bus rests.

Now on the sidewalk I chew
a useless toothpick taking in
the swiss chalet railroad depot,
remembering the noodles in my chicken

soup.

Outside this town it must be wild
to make these broken men, brittle
women. They chew gum as if the mines
could work again, as if it was *me*.

No jukebox or beer will save you
tonight in Portland. All night
the radio will come through the wall.
Listen, we could meet in Wallace,

go to a room where the lamp is busted.

Conspiracy In Iowa

There are some very ghastly faces
pressed against my windows
these nights and something
big has been in the potatoes.

Have you ever been to Lone Tree?
Where a bloody man sells
geese and leaves their heads
by his pump till they're skulls?

There is a man in Iowa who keeps
Pancho Villa's skull in a leather
trunk with mementos from Japan,
a small portrait of his mother.

Out here where a dog's tongue sticks
to his own frozen water, catfish
winter sullenly under the ice,
moving their tails in long, slow thrashes.

Where faces watch my wife undress
and there is nothing in my mailbox
but letters with windows, or a ladybug,
or an ad for Farm/Sport Thermal Sox.

And if you've ever been to Tipton
you know they don't have parking meters,
but four saloons, a courthouse, three
variety stores, a hippie and a movie theatre.

And I tell you there's trouble
right here in Iowa City when a boy
would stand the cold, far from
parental love, T.V., to see us enjoy

one legal pleasure in this wretched land.

CARD BURNING IN CENTRAL PARK

I open my family magazine, pretty
girls, whiskey bottles and then you.
I show my wife. She says you're a troll,
your teeth look crooked and why do I
run around with fuck-ups like you anyway?
Some questions don't expect answers.

Mountains and bad weather have done
something for me, I feel my Wheaties.
They're crunchy and the morning paper
clues me in on Ed Slocum's lost cows.
Last night a canyon wind blew over
gas war signs, drove magpies into town.

I know you're unfit for service,
even the cops won't beat you publicly,
but old-timers can pick out desperadoes.
Out there in the sheep meadow with
Mad Dog Anderson, your eyes like Saturday
night, you cup the flame to a cheroot.

TRUMANSBURG FAIR

In her little tent Honey Bumps
lumbered out of sequin finery,
cymbals banging each victory.
We stood, tanned and drunk
in the dark pit, feeling handsome.
A loudspeaker announced cattle.

That lady's rubber dummy had
a wink, a leer, a cocked hat,
and a name I've since forgotton.
That man boards my bus at
night, thumbs my magazine,
is only cigar smoke at dawn.

We finger our girls in the
House of Fun, weird laughter
and blackness made us private.
The firemen's beer made us dizzy
in the sun while farmers with
beasts trampled chaos everywhere.

Our world swung wide
on the corners as we slept;
only stars hung over
the lake and pastureland.
We woke heavy-headed before
the city, holding our rumpled girls.

TAUGHANNOCK FALLS

Forty-five thousand tons of ice
and melting. When that pillar
crashes it will be spring around here.

When it's going well it thuds
into the pool continuously, a pro-
longed thud that tourists confuse

with echo. When it's not so well
it spurts, like an old man finishing
off a pee, shaking it out.

Maybe for kicks these falls should
have phosphorous as some boats
do at night in certain seas.

Whole families would wait
for dusk and go ooh and ahh
as the wonderful sparks flow

down lighting faces of sleeping kids.
Some damnfools would stick around
till very late to swim in diamonds.

Our Trip South

We thought they were hawks.
We admired their size and
graceful circles but near Meridian
we saw them eating a dead turtle.

It was just like the books and movies.
Waitresses said y'all and everywhere
old darkies rocked and watched us pass
with shabby, careless eyes.

It was nothing we knew.
The distant tire peel grew into
a dead armadillo and was gone
so fast we had to talk about it.

The passion we saw was air conditioners.
roaring like morgue machines they
drove us stalking wild again and again
into the night where a real air

enveloped us and like those great bugs
we battered sullenly back to light.

TALK IN LOUISIANA

for Richard Kilbourne

The giant spider is like an aerialist
panicked and clutching at his rope.
Actually it is a pregnant she, resting.
Notice how the trunks of these little
trees resemble the arms of old Dwarves.
Air sits thick around us as if the sea
were here; bad for bad lungs.
You see the tropic plants that turn
to mush, consistency of cooked greens
at the first frost; the way oysters color.
Under the continents channels run
and great oceans warmed by friction
of the settling earth contain dark
monstrous shapes that move unseen.
Our bitter poison brings them up.
When lions ate men in England
Phoenicians saw them floating huge
and awful even dead and hugged the shore.
They thought frightened apes were men
but who can say that they were wrong?
Strange tales come to us from woodcutters
of Silesia, Yugoslavia, Manchuria.
And our bodies seem spongy, there
is this neurotic drive for peace,
children without appetite. . .

THE FLORIDA WINTER

1

They used hunks of raw fish
for bait and caught groupers
but I only got a jellyfish.
There were people so old they
couldn't even tan anymore
and a couple sleazy pelicans
that lived on hamburgers.
Hitchhiking back to Tampa
a man told me to live clean,
keep away from whores who
are everywhere and after pretty
young fellows like myself.

2

A block of expensive homes
smashed by the storm, full
of tropical debris and water
is visited by the newsreel team.
The camera pauses to note
that a mahogany stereo heaped
with lesser trash will play no more.
Here is a man with flowers on
his shirt having a drink
on what is left of his veranda.
His deoderant has worn off
but he for one, will rebuild.
With pudgy fingers full of rings
he rubs his eyes wearily.

3

After saving his wife from drowning,
I drank scotch with a retired
policeman from Boston, Massachusetts.
The story of his life was long,
uncomplicated; the scotch good.
He took his shoe and sock off
in the Everglades Club bar to show
me how a lawnmower snipped him.
Florida was his kind of place
and the missus liked it too.

Chinese Again

1

I too can barely stand
my loneliness
and my excellence.

But I have nothing of jade
and in spring I smell
dog offal,
not jasmine.

This wind brings tears
though I have no tower.
My nose bleeds
inscrutable red petals.

The elephant fountain
rainbows
my misery
in its dismal trickle.

2

As maple leaves commence
to stink under the snow
how I yearn
for her supple sweat!

As this barbarian wind
sucks into my little house
I hear her caterpillar pads
inching to my room.

You can hear my heart
squealing and hissing
to a stop.
Cocks crow, dogs bark,
children laugh but wise
men throw stones
where the bear dances
without a master.

LIZARDS

We hear rubber tires mostly
in these Southern towns.
Spent gasoline is in every bite.
But lizards are my daily symbol,
changing colors in the sun.
The satanic eyes cock so
the view is unbalanced chaos,
stillness flashing to hysteria.
The lizard in the vine is green
and the brown one keeps his paw
in an anthill. Single-mindedness
is the secret of lizards and me too.
The lizard you catch is a tail
squirming in your disgusted fist
and in this "riot of colors" flowers
are clubbing me to silence.

RIGHT FIELD

Shoo dragonflies with your mitt,
work up a sweat straddle-hopping.
What you notice out here is clover
and clouds bloating out in the sky.
The long walk in to the dust.

A start right, two jumps, hard
run to the scoop, stop, flip, throw
and you stand sweating, blood in your ears.
Looking up, Mother is letting loose
Dad's ashes a good 70 miles from the gulf.

Some guys kiss the bat, mud their hands,
spit, and wink at a girl. Then they hit it.
It's a sweet thing in your stomach when
the ball lifts out of the world, sighing
into the arms of an amazed urchin.

Every ball was in the sun when Father
watched me play. It's still out here
where the razz competes with a bumblebee.
Soft floater against the clouds, easy
bounder for a toss to first and hunkered

again in stinky grass I raise my glove.
Mother hovers in her piper cub
and Father, of course, is not a star,
not cheering, or laughing, looking.
Blue eyes drifting between some clouds.

COUGH

Every cough echoes off walls
of a ghost town: down black
holes that were silver mines.
Spittle for the weeds. Patient
burro in the shadows of vultures.

plodding down an old rut
humming a tune for the horny
toads--Mm kiss me, kiss me wa
wa. Hello, what's this? White
man's bones. Time for a snort

old girl, smack gums for luck.
Now back in Louisiana I'd get
them hacking fits and birds would
zoom out of the cane and right back
again. Some damn tired birds there.

Those peppers'll ruin your estomacko
too. Eat like a bunch of Zunis down there.
Hard times everywhere these days, nothing
to laugh at but your own farts or little
dust devils tickling your ass when you squat.

My little burro must think me queer,
no television or religion, humming
kiss me, coughing my gristle to pulp.
Just sit in this ditch and clatter
a tune on the ribs with a bone.

Cold Sweat

*Betelgeuse—"A variable red giant
star of the first magnitude, near
one shoulder of Orion"* Webster's
New Collegiate Dictionary 1956

There are three brittle flies
in a pop bottle where you sit
in the attic and the air
is chalk and cheap cement.

Outside it pretends to be
Texas; distant rumbles
north, monotony of frog
chorus screaming in the marsh.

You come down to our porch
in a stranger's wedding gown.
You're moist and soft in twilight
with cobwebs streaked in your flush.

Oh let's never fight like this again.
The night is liquid as always
and there is mine called beetle-juice.
Your star is a whispered secret.

Late tonight while the machines
groan out the cold I'll be awake.
Then I'll wipe these cold drops
again and fight your dreams till dawn.

Little House On The Great Plains

The first night rats trundled
through the walls, Hilda
cried and kept the baby in bed.
He laid out poison and they died.
One thrashing and screaming
in the basement, the rest
between partitions. Hilda
couldn't stand the smell.
He knocked the walls out
and found a chestful of money.
They paid off the car and bought
the sailboat he'd always wanted.
The boy's dog keeps the rats out
now, the neighbors are very nice
for the most part, and Hilda
is real busy making the house
into a home for all of them.

Poem

This poem is called
The Electrocution of an Elephant.
It is about movies
where jerky people jerk around,
abruptly fading and reappearing.
Here the mayor is making a speech
about electricity.
He points at the elephant with his cigar.
A gentleman from the electric company
pulls a switch, completing the circuit.
First the front right leg crumples,
then the left, the backside topples,
a few spasms and the beast is still.
It's quite a sight.
Of course the smell of singed flesh
does not pervade the air
because in those early years
the cameraman's art was not fully realized.
So when the men in top hats
and ladies with parasols jerk
down the platform steps,
the last curious onlooker waddles off,
we're left with this elephant
for about twenty seconds.

II

GRASSHOPPER'S SONG

For my child's amusement
I can roll out a few snowmen
on Saturday while the world
goes unchecked to hell
outside my yard.

To cheer a confused friend
I can pick at the asylum's chairarm
for an hour or so and leave false-
faced, reminded too late of news
to tell, on a Sunday.

And I spend my days assailed
by thoughts I can't remember,
like baseballs from a pitching machine,
absorbed in nothing like other men
who start their lives on Monday.

With no malice for well-fed
women collecting money for the poor,
I can be too full to eat dessert,
knowing my father's basement
is cluttered with broken toys.

Week after week I prance and clown,
heedless of the shifting wind
that makes the hands of dour
men frantic, but know with
sadness I see doors shut, one by one.

Waking Up Dead

Thunder was clapping
in the wings outside the window.
With every last word
we smelled his spoiled liver.
It filled the room
where the dying man yearned
for just one dangling cobweb
to ease the boredom of his end.

One more poet down,
killed young in the daylight,
cries of women echoing on linoleum.
And the town progresses normally,
invisible spirits mingling with umbrellas.
Too early for a beer, too late for lunch,
the taxi drops us to face alone
a rainy day in our empty houses.

How did I forget how
to grieve strongly at these final losses?
Depressed arrangements on the telephone,
ginger back-pats, limp tired face
that is a white man's blues.

Dozing at the matinee I hear
again the radio voice praising our dead.
I see my grandmother come on the porch
tired from the kitchen.
She is squinting without her glasses.
She dries her hands on the flag
and opens her mouth to call me.
I wake suddenly in the thick air
and everywhere children are screaming,
throwing things in the dark.

Way Out On The Ice

I've never seen these trees
this way before.
It's as if I'm on a white sand
desert. I hardly dare to walk.
It's as if I'm in a movie.
The moon and the fish beneath
me can't talk. Only I know
what a fool I am tonight.
I know I am a walker where
I once swam, under
this bridge in a silver path.
I may come from between
these gorge walls screaming,
waving arms, blind in the light.

EXPLAINING SNOW

Off snow the air is bright
and often only your face is cold
while the rest of you sweats.
Little girls trudging home
from school in snow sometimes
get so tired they begin to cry
and go to bed immediately.

Every snowflake, like fingerprints,
is different but in February
when you are twenty-six
this is no longer interesting.
In warm weather snow is heavier.
It rarely snows in very cold weather.
When it warms, then cools, snow crusts.

Around wool fibers snow forms ice
balls that grow with contact.
Children make snow angels by lying
flat and sweeping their arms.
All this causes sodden clothes, painful
chapping which in later years becomes
"the weather-beaten New England look."

Snow is essential to the Yankee life.
Without snow it is pointless to lie
to your children, build a fire,
get tipsy with relatives you despise
or pretend confidence in a human God.
To not know snow is to miss
the religious excitement of your warmth.

Conquistador

What were they?
Dispossessed nobles looking for gold,
businessmen hoping for big stuff
to make the country club a reality
for the kids. Also professional soldiers
and homosexual sailors expecting nothing.

What did they find?
Puritanical savages who slaughtered
usable virgins for a few paltry maize crops.
There was lots of gold but the government
got most of it, but it was nice being a god
on the days it was cool and didn't rain.

Historical significance?
For a while the Chesapeake round-up
was fun but local appeal ended that.
Every year a couple of green coins wash
up on hotel beaches and in Mexico
some people are proud of being a little whiter.

Well, what about us?
Think of some beautiful diarrhetic madman
wandering through Florida, drinking everything
to preserve his youth.

ABOUT SONG MY, SINCE YOU ASK

When those yahoos shot those boys
in Mississippi I imagine
at least one yahoo was smiling.
I tend to think it was
an "embarrassed smile"
though it was probably dark
and no one was looking at anyone else.

Just see *yourself* out in the woods,
all that stupid moss in the trees,
knowing you're going to die.
Shit! I really did it this time!
All those dimestore loafers so excited
they're forgetting and slapping
their boils, drinking too fast.

Brush your teeth but your breath
stinks. So you chew gum.
You sweat, your hair cream
won't work, your wife sleeps
around. Your girl does too.
Best goddam country in the world
and all you've got is pimples and a hurt.

Those boys over in the Nam
didn't want to die either.
It was hot, they were scared.
All those ugly slime screaming
and pleading in gobbledegook
for their lives. If you shoot mamma-
san, you have to shoot the kids too.

It's the secret fear, unspoken truth
that twists the heart to any frenzy.

III

FOR DICK HUGO

This fat man murders
all the women he loves.
He holds them underwater
so long they become trout
and they cover his face with tiny kisses.
We would watch some ballgames
and drink some drinks and outside
a sunset burned like an ulcer in the mountain.
He should live in a shotgun house
so when he threw open his arms
everything would collapse.
Boom! "Hey, my house has fallen
into lumber at my feet."
And that is the only art there is.
So sometimes when I'm drunk
and sitting in the kitchen by streetlight
this man comes barging into my heart,
sweating, like he was my father or something.

Farewell To Dwight Eisenhower

> "*Something tells me we aren't
> in Kansas anymore, Toto.*"
> —The Wizard of Oz

Tonight we're falling all over
in love with ourselves.
We're kissing strangers, forgetting
our dogs tied to parking meters,
whining at the dusty moon.

And when the bars close us out
we waltz in the empty street
singing Chuck Berry smoky-mouthed,
the hounds gone mad at our heels,
knowing the first man on that rare moon

will say the view is real lovely,
ask for the Army-Navy score.
We may awake tomorrow on a bony
couch to the sound of a woman
frying bacon with all her might.

Leaving this deafening grief past
the inscrutable cruelty of sunglasses
and pimples, past the dog grinning
from its newspaper grave we may
pass into the fumes of this thirsty

city with the calm knowledge
of history and clean underwear.

JEHOVAH'S WITNESS CALLER

She looked so cold,
varicose-veined, I said come in
please. Would you like some tea?
No, thank you. I didn't either.
What do you think about the wickedness
in the world today?
I'm a Roman Catholic I said.
She read the titles of her magazine
articles to me. I asked
if she wanted some tea then.
She went away.
I wanted to ask if she
really wanted to kill all the queers.
I wanted to tell her
about my grand-dad who was a J. W.
How my asshole Methodist relatives
think I'm crazy like he was.
How he used to hitchhike
all over the country spreading
the Word, selling poison ivy
and blister balm.
The wicked world assaults
me like the liquor I drink.
Sometimes Christ is so near
I tremble corn flakes on my paper.
I want no heart, or blood,
but my own, brave lady.

LETTER

Lying in a hammock at
summer's end in Connecticut
reading Benvenuto Cellini,
I saw you for the last time.
We colored in your picture
books or played scrabble
with your sister when it rained.
It was understood that
I should win my share.
There was a lake with snaky
weeds that tangled in our legs.
Copperheads lived in the rocks
and we took a flashlight
when walking after dinner.
You worked where mysterious
weapons are made and, sworn

to secrecy, joked yet were silent.
I was sick, laughing too loudly,
and nervous lay awake at night.
Sometimes in bed with the
light out I talk to my wife
who listens and brings beer.
She would like to hear about
you, but I speak of Cellini
until we finally sleep.

The Boy In The River

Do the carp nibble your toes?
Or is this a hideous way
to keep borrowed records?
Does your old girlfriend say
Oh, I should have let him,
and feel a little older?
Every morning as I hit your
bridge coughing the first cigarette
I look for you, in the debris.
It makes my day when you aren't
tangled in some root or crate.
Tell me, can you have your cake
and eat it? I believe in you.

THEY GIVE ME YOUR IMAGE

for James Welch

Some child has chewed your face
but you are redman, no mistake.
Knees bent, feet wide in wardance
even if your spear is half-eaten.

Last night I drank like a blue Pict
while the moon ate me for dinner.
This morning the black kids
brought you where I trembled.

I am a squat white man, cold
in the dew, clutching an image
under the sky where unseen stars
go furiously toward nothing.

There are few like this left but
I will stamp and shriek proud
madness, hug trees for loving.
I will daub my body with tree shit.

Children will play with my magic
teeth, my bones will frighten man.
When my kind last screamed in battle
Roman legions fouled themselves and won.

Of course you are not a plastic toy.
You are Pigeon. You sing songs.
There are Warriors, wise men, doctors,
but I am kept because not to is unlucky.

Trip To The Firetower

for Rob Patton

The Indians who lived here once
were cruel and smart.
They wintered together in bark longhouses
and tortured one another mercilessly.
The trails they used were made by deer,
and they were sent away long ago.

Drab women and ugly children
gape numbly from their trailers
as we tool along up the road.
But the men never look up
from their truck engines.
They don't even stamp a cold foot.

I feel like I belong out here
wrapped in my gray coat like a big rat.
Your red beard and the pretty blonde
girl are out of place and should go.
I would stand alone, a dismal statue
in the white snow, among bare, black limbs.

But you don't and we climb
the firetower to where it's really cold.
At the top the door is locked as if
they just don't care about fires anymore.
So we look up and down the valley.
The oaks a little higher and apart

as if they were harder to cut down
once. Easier to plow around than chop.
As it was easier once for Indians to bathe
cold toes in their own warm piss hunched
by the homefire, or follow a deer trail
as the way down. And the stillness

of this light snow we keep apace
eases me and seems so natural.

STETHOSCOPE

for Thom Burton

Can you make pictures
of what you hear?
We do not strain to make
the jumbled noise below
come clear but tease our words
to fit this room, our lives.

These canvas chairs can never
learn our shapes but our old
lies linger on our tongues
like the good wine we never
could afford, and never missed.
Outside cold night shapes this house.

But put that instrument
to your chest again to listen to
the thump and gurgle that is you.
It's good to hear the things
that makes us go, fearful
that we may see them.

If my fingers worked the way
they should I'd play a clavichord,
or fix my own bad faucets.
You don't hang your pictures
about your house the way
I cudgel flowers with my voice.

What is most fine though
is this common thundering.
The junco birds in the pine tree,
the tall beer, the silence.
Those consistent thwacks within,
each as different as snowflakes.

KILLING TIME

for my brother and my sister

Since I can't decide which way to go
others choose and I'm always in the middle.
I loved your cats, your parakeets,
but couldn't bring myself to own my own.
We're certainly all fucked up now.

There I was for a while chucking stones
in the river, sipping a small jar I'd
saved, worrying about you. The stupid
chinook kept blowing hair in my eyes.
How come you guys never worry about me?

Too busy with your butterflies, your freeze-
dried coffee, your bills, your bonsai
trees, your smart-ass friends with yachts
is why. I have a brother who is drunk
and writes poetry to kill time you say.

He's everything I'm not but just like me
you try to say. Smart but never wins,
lazy but his work will make him great.
Screwy. What you mean to say is
please like me everyone. Please like *me*.

That's the way I'd like it now, striding
past these white farmhouses with dogs
strangling on their chains to get a taste
of me. To clutch a drink in the kitchen
of some party, jovial, red-faced, vulnerable.

CHEKHOV AND MUSSOLINI'S ROSE

for Walter Slatoff

This evening my spirit
is leaving my body.
It travels on the voices
of lawnmowers, settles
in the twigs of old birdhouses.
Soon it is all gone, dis-
solved. Odor of terror and flesh.

Now look at this child blistered
by fire, alive and screaming
in the strange arms of a corpse.
Certainly this is where Chekhov
leaves and we turn to curled things.
The boiled crab, baboons "traumatized"
for science, dry spiders dangling.

This morning at the lunch counter
there was no moderation. Perhaps
there are no children in our country.
No young hand waiting on the edge
of the hospital sheet. Only hard
voices muttering as if through fever,
life flashing like a ptomaine Visual.

Listen, Slatoff, I am *Il Duce*.
I am so young, so passionately
unready. My lovely wife, my
poor babies. My binoculars see
all the action. Even you. And
it's not so bad, it's all we've got.
This hideous rose blooming,
uncurling with timeless beauty.

After A Memorial Service

I suspect it was the rain
that killed you. You
went slow to be safe
and got hit from behind.

They read what they said
were your favorite poems.
They said a lot of other things too,
but we didn't believe that shit either.

If your soul could sing
like those hungry morning birds,
travel like a September wind,
it would be enough for us.

But it doesn't. We will live
until we die and then we'll be dead.
That certainly is the terror
and the dignity of our grief.

Your death collects the sadness
of this year, brings on another season.
That is all in memory we can give
and if what was said was true

We would not have come.

ELEGY

for Tony Woodward

He wrote notes in his Bible,
studied yoga and boxing.
One sub-zero night we saw
him out running in gym shorts.
Everyone knew he slept on the floor.

I was an early morning tennis
partner in his schedule (one hour
for meditation, girls, great books)
and I think he rather liked me.
Liberalism was a cause of his.

Voted most likely to fuck-up,
I did and so did he eventually.
While I was a drunkard and a liar
he went respectably mad, and abroad.
Nothing had changed except ourselves.

I see him tromping through the Alps,
lunging in mountain air, musing
on nature's majesty and mortal souls.
He was no sickly poet destined for
early death. He was a more real fool.

It's too easy to say the world's shitty
when we really hate ourselves so I'll
say I liked him, and feel cheated now.
When friends die we get jealous with
our grief and touch ourselves for luck.

SLIM

My wife's Uncle Slim from Circle
Montana has six weeks to live.
In this town I walk to work,
through woods, by a lake.
Frogs splat off as I pass, green
is the only word going this season.
I'm a moving cancer in paradise
today. My life is so incomparable
with a bird song, or cowboys.
Slim was at our wedding with his
wide lapels and when he grinned
my knees grew firm, my smile fixed.
He never wore any bandana or
silver spurs either. He came from Norway.
He had one son and a sick wife.
I know nothing about farming because
my father was a teacher but I know
woods and today I feel so terrible.

Epithalamium For Michael And Gail Lynch

Ah, how her blush becomes her.
His knees are signalling distant friends.
Her hands are peaceful as in sleep,
his pants are filled with the wind.
What have we joined asunder today?

Obnoxious rice doomed to drown
in the usual wedding rain,
car horns, bloody sheets, and groans
of lost love in the farthest pew?
Wise advice gets a chaste bride's kiss.

So they've up and done it,
the fatal plunge, mixing it up.
Now comes the broken washer,
I thought I told you, dirty tub
and kids, who make you kiss in secret.

What a great day to eat food,
merrily bullshit the time away.
Tonight I may dedicate a drunk
to those newly wed hoping
they recognize happiness.

SOMETIMES

Hardy: *You've never met my wife, have you?*
Laurel: *Yes, I've never met her.*

Sometimes my tongue only talks
to the back of my teeth.
I'm speaking to you,
but you can't hear me.
Sometimes my teeth are like
a very great and famous wall in China.

Being philosophical as if I'm in the woods
with a bunch of scouts is o.k.
for otherwise. I'm sorry
I'm drunk when I say good things.
Goat-eyes with a choking snake
voice. Grasping like a capsized beetle.

Yes, it's the beauty that gets me
crazy these days. Seasons
falling into place with a slow
grandeur, touching you in each one.
Touching your children,
their tiny ribs, their pulsing innards.

Sometimes my words echo back
and talk to me all night.
I admit my teeth are bad, my breath
stinks, then I won't respond.
My hands open and shut,
open and close. My arms

zig-zag in the dark trying
to catch you.

Love Poem

Down the street where the pharmacy light
swings alone on its hinges the wind comes
and shakes our house till its teeth rattle
all night as we lie together in the same bed.

Do the hawks that we see wheeling overhead,
or the burrowing mice sleep in these gales?
The geese must fly over the storm, little things
must huddle close to somebody nice at night.

There it goes again and any moment now we're
off to Oz. Hogs and chickens thud off the house
for a while, thin whistling slugs of rain try
to kill us as we mingle toes in our fort.

Tunnels in the high levees that Indians built
or picket fences by the highway department
can't save us as we hurtle away inside each
other with the hawks and the mice and the hogs.

Roses

Well, the first petal
has fallen from her birthday rose.
Soon they'll be dripping off
in odorous little bunches.

Fortunately girls aren't roses
and that thorn beneath the bloom
business doesn't whet up
too much in me.

Flesh isn't malleable,
and that's what's nice about it.
Crashing about all night,
coming, going, talking,

eating breakfast.

JAPANESE MOVIE

Hynagh! goes the bad guy
and struts and grunts about
the peasant's corpse.
Then the good guy who is searching
his kidnapped sweetheart
slices him down and eventually
finds her in a bandit's cave.
A rockslide brings them eternally
together. Hynagh! I go
in the parking lot.
Stop being an ass says my wife.

HAND WRINGING

Today I walked in bitter wind
like a cold nail in my brain, grinding
teeth shamelessly at the success of others.
Once home I saw my hands spread
red and stumpy on the tablecloth
as if they'd done some noble labor once.
One set of fingers bent from bicycling
into parked cars; arthritic, scarred
by childish habits, drinking accidents.
Like the bumpy nose and dysentery
they testify those dear failures in my life.
I should stop this insomniac cringing
in the night, give my family the love
they deserve and slink around my chair to get.

FOR THE DEAD ONES

This is Valentine's day and I'm
thinking about every one
of you. Now you're gone
I love you. Please be mine.

It was Saturday all day today
and your faces came to me
so clearly, so suddenly,
the beer went warm in my mouth.

Here are my children, two boys.
My wife is in the kitchen.
Why do you call me out
tonight? Your living eyes,

as if I could just pick up
the phone and end this misery.
We will never see each other
again. Not ever again.

IV

Practical Pig

(a confessional poem)

They said I must be practical,
constrain myself against myself.
When I had tantrums then the old
house creaked, my dinner went
dusty on my plate and I guess
I broke their hearts to bits.

But I've had to build this life
I'm living. The drinks, all these
lonely movies, my tense jaws
trying to work up an audible whine.
Christ! All these religious drinks
to dull and feed my hungry love.

And every time I look in a mirror,
like right now, at my drunk and
tear-stained face I know what I am.
I'm practical. Practical Pig.
And I always feel a little triumphant.

SQUANTO

Lift up the flap
and there is Jack-in-his-pulpit.
Those quiet sexy flowers of spring,
so moving after a hard winter.
Makes me think of Squanto.
Good old Squanto so fond
of tobacco and a good fire.
Just squatting by the hearth
smelling bad, grinning at everybody.
He planted his corn with fish
and yanked down squirrels
by their tails. When he slept
he dreamt of flowers, his mouth
fell open and they saw his missing teeth.
He slept outside in case he should die
and he loved to touch the soft white children.

GUN SHELLS

Luckily there was an old duck blind.
So we sat and smoked as the trees
grew wonderfully green across the lake.
Too sleepy for talk we just listened
to the rain splatter between cattails.
Later, when frogs were building their
twilight roar, and I was stepping
into the car I saw the earth glitter.
And with a nagging sadness I was
back in my own bed in pajamas,
my parents muffled voices below,
gunshells dribbling through my fingers
like money, totally contented.

Twilight At City Park

The radio goes Big-Beat
and the park swings in twilight.
Little Russell starts his impolite
but beautiful bumps while the kids
on the old oak limb hambone along.
Hands, shoulders, glistening heads
coax and jive in the settling night.
Now just the eyes of fire; a sense
more fluid and correct than this smell
of rotting flowers, this great river
giving its pestilence to the sea.

Sledding On Monday

When I pull the kid
on his sled up the hill
I taste last night's cigarettes.
When we go down
it's different.
Sledding down the hill
where I used to sled,
this time alone on the slope.
Just me and my boy.
I keep feeling like Slim Pickens
riding a bomb to Moscow.
You having fun? Wanna
go home? I ask each time
we land and he just lies
in the snow and laughs
and laughs.

For Nathaniel

Her bag-of-waters broke
and it started to snow.
Ten minutes at the hospital
and she gives me a boy.
What will I do with
all these boys that rock
and roll out of her womb?
Will I sympathize with pimples,
flying lessons, feet on the table,
or worse? These snowballs
I'm making won't pack.
Just a dirty clump of snow.
You've got to have red little hands
to make good snowballs.
You've got to *care* about snowballs
with snow like this and I don't.
I feel too excellent,
untouchable.

About Kindly Old Geppeto, Said P.

Surely men have lived in stomachs
of whales and told the truth.
If I refer to elders as wise
it's to help you like this story.

I've been a real boy for a while
now but that emptiness returns.
Walking the midway this morning
I smelled footlong dogs

and heard the power engine though
it was still as the middle of oak.
Come to me feeling of birth,
brief freshness of toothpaste.

It's not the big wheel turning
in the sunset for me but a candle
guttering. Great ancient beasts
powering under continents in silence.

I did it for the old man, the bird
and the cat. They were so afflicted
by dark and dank; aching mortal bones.
For this I was blessed and drifted.

All day I sit next to giant rats
from the sewers of Paris, France.

Reddy Fox: Some Notes Toward A Theory Of Tragedy

The sign on the cage said "Reddy"
and inside a fox slept all day.
It was the end of an illusion.

If only our dreams were ordered!
If it was anguish instead of boredom
that peculiar pain we feel in the zoo

would be less uncomfortable.
You see, Chicken Little, Turkey
Lurkey and all those had a tragic flaw--

stupidity compounded by naive idealism.
We lie to children because it's fun.
Yes, that fox was indeed very naughty.

The children are afraid of the sleeping fox;
they identify with gingerbread men
and dependent farmyard little folk.

Because I'm a grown-up I think
it would be funny if the fox gobbled
up the pimply teenager who is poking him.

I'd split my sides if he licked his chops
afterward and held his bulging tummy.
Just buttons, belt buckle and a greasy comb left.

Just dreams, idle philosophy to carry
me past the pus-eyed antelopes.